ECONOMIC AND SOCIAL COMMISSION FOR ASIA AND THE PACIFIC

MANAGING THE TRANSITION FROM THE VILLAGE TO THE CITY IN THE SOUTH PACIFIC

UNITED NATIONS
New York, 1999

ST/ESCAP 1994

UNITED NATIONS PUBLICATION

Sales No. E.00.II.F.48

Copyright © United Nations 2000

ISBN: 92-1-119997-2

Copies of this publication may be obtained from:

ESCAP/UNCHS Joint Section on Human Settlements
Population and Rural and Urban Development Division
Economic and Social Commission for Asia and the Pacific
United Nations Building
Rajdamnern Nok Avenue
Bangkok 10200

Fax: (66-2) 288 1097

E-mail: <huset.unescap@un.org>

ACKNOWLEDGEMENTS

This publication was prepared for the United Nations by Utkatu Naiker, visiting faculty member at Queensland University. The funding for the study was provided by the United Nations Development Programme. The secretariat wishes to acknowledge the contributions of the UNDP regional office in Fiji, the Asia-Pacific Office of the United Nations Centre for Human Settlements, the ESCAP Pacific Operations Centre, the Asian Development Bank and the South Pacific Forum Secretariat in reviewing the drafts of this publication and providing valuable comments, corrections and additions.

CONTENTS

Tables

Boxes

PREFACE

As we enter the twenty-first century, one of the key emerging issues in Asia and the Pacific region is urbanization. In the next few years, for the first time in human history, more people will be living in cities and towns than in villages. While the positive and negative impacts of urbanization, and its linkages to economic development, environment, poverty and globalization, have been and are being examined fairly extensively for most Asian countries, the transition from villages to towns in the Pacific island countries has, to a great extent, remained an issue of low priority. One of the reasons for this neglect is that, compared to the sheer magnitude of the demographic transition in Asia in terms of the numbers involved the process of urbanization in the Pacific island countries appears miniscule. However, the impact of urbanization on these countries is as severe and, in some cases, more severe than on Asian countries. Because of their small land mass and population size and their distance from global markets, Pacific island countries cannot benefit from the external economies or the economies of scale that most Asian countries enjoy. Policy approaches to address urbanization in these countries therefore have to be different.

This publication outlines the unique features of urbanization and urban problems in the developing countries of the South Pacific. It also suggests possible approaches to address those issues. An abridged version of this publication was presented, as an issue paper, to the South Pacific Forum Economic Ministers Meeting, held at Apia, Samoa, in July 1999. After reviewing the paper, the Meeting endorsed a proposal to convene an expert group meeting to prepare an action agenda on human settlements in the Pacific based on the Global Plan of Action in the Habitat Agenda of 1996 and the Regional Action Plan on Urbanization of 1993.

INTRODUCTION

The pattern of human settlements is changing rapidly in the South Pacific, with increasing numbers of people moving to live in towns and cities. The populations of the major urban areas in most countries are growing faster than national populations. The rates of urban growth in Solomon Islands and Vanuatu, both in excess of 6 per cent per annum, are among the highest in the world.

One of the effects of such rapid urban growth is that the availability of basic services such as water supply, sanitation, waste disposal, housing, schools, health and recreational facilities is worsening for many poor residents. Informal and squatter settlements are growing as more migrants come to seek a living in the towns. In atolls such as Betio in South Tarawa and Ebeye in the Marshall Islands, the carrying capacity of the land is stretched to the limit. In larger urban centres such as Port Moresby and Suva, poverty, unemployment and crime rates have been rising constantly. Government institutions at the national and local levels, as well as the traditional leadership structures, have been unable to manage the transition from village to cities efficiently.

At the global level, these issues were addressed at the United Nations Conference on Human Settlements (Habitat II), held in 1996, which followed the United Nations conferences on environment, small islands, population, social development and women. Habitat II produced the Habitat Agenda, including a Global Plan of Action that focused on ways and means of ensuring adequate shelter for all and managing sustainable human settlements in an urbanizing world. The Ministerial Conference on Urbanization in Asia and the Pacific, organized by ESCAP in 1993, formulated a Regional Action Plan on Urbanization. The broad coverage of these plans of action needs to be supplemented by more specific subregional plans and programmes.

Many countries in the South Pacific have common urban features and problems. For most, urbanization is a modern phenomenon, which is being managed through a mixture of western and traditional socio-cultural systems. All are attempting to resolve the constraints on the development of customary land. There is insufficient information flow on the current progress being made in the region and opportunities are limited to learn from the valuable experience acquired over many decades in the planning, development and management of urban settlements in the region. Regional cooperation also needs to be strengthened to improve the response to urban growth, particularly in terms of policies for the provision of infrastructure, housing, land and urban management, through the adoption of sound urban governance practices, best suited to the socio-economic and cultural systems common in the South Pacific.

This overview identifies the major issues in urban management in the South Pacific developing countries and suggests options for action at the national and regional levels. The Pacific countries are at different stages in national and urban development. However, there are some common areas for improving the response to urban growth. The major elements are as follows:

- The need for a positive approach to urbanization in national development planning.

- The need for effective urban governance.

- Urban planning to coordinate and integrate development proposals.

- Implementation mechanisms for infrastructure, housing and land supply.

- Public participation and human resources development.

The key recommendations, as summarized in Part Two, could be considered for application as stated or with appropriate adaptation to suit specific situations. These were considered at the South Pacific Forum Economic Ministers Meeting, held in Apia on 1 and 2 July 1999. The Meeting instructed the Forum Secretariat to consult other regional bodies with a view to developing a subregional plan of action based on the Habitat Agenda and the Regional Action Plan on Urbanization, but reflecting the circumstances of the Pacific island countries.

PART ONE

OVERVIEW OF HUMAN SETTLEMENTS AND URBANIZATION

I. URBANIZATION: A NEW PHENOMENON IN THE SOUTH PACIFIC

Rapid urbanization is a feature of human settlements globally and the United Nations estimates that, by the year 2000, almost 50 per cent of the world population will be living in urban areas. The Asian and Pacific region contains three-fifths of the world's population and also a large and increasing share of its economic activities and its urban population (UNCHS 1996a).

Urbanization is strongly correlated with economic development. Evidence from many developing countries indicates that an increasing proportion of the national gross domestic product is produced in urban areas. This is not surprising if one considers the fact that goods and services produced in towns and cities benefit from external economies and economies of scale, and enjoy better terms of trade compared with goods produced in rural areas. The United Nations Conference on Human Settlements (Habitat II), held in Istanbul, Turkey, in June 1996, drew attention to the growth of cities, their role in national economic, social and physical development and key issues in managing the process of urbanization. It formulated the Habitat Agenda as a global plan of action to address those issues.

The South Pacific region of developing countries extending from Papua New Guinea to Cook Islands and from Niue to the Marshall Islands accounted for a population of some 7 million in 1997 (for example, Melanesia 5.9 million, Polynesia 600,000 and Micronesia 500,000). The region comprises Melanesia, which covers Fiji, Papua New Guinea, Solomon Islands, and Vanuatu; Polynesia, which covers Cook Islands, Niue, Samoa, Tokelau and Tonga; and Micronesia, which covers the Federated States of Micronesia, Kiribati, the Marshall Islands, Nauru and Tuvalu.

All the countries in the South Pacific have always had one or more urban centres which have served as major administrative and commercial hubs and which have provided a higher level of educational and health services than rural centres. However, urbanization is a recent phenomenon in many countries. The faster rate of growth of urban areas and the transition from living in villages to living in towns is creating unusual and difficult situations for the new urban dwellers, as well as for national and local governments and the traditional leadership structures.

Owing to lack of planning and investment, the physical pattern of urban development is often haphazard and environmental degradation is growing. Many of the major urban centres in the South Pacific are showing the same symptoms of rapid urbanization as those in other developing countries.

This chapter briefly describes the major aspects of urbanization in the developing countries of the South Pacific region. The countries covered are all members of the South Pacific Forum, the major intergovernmental body coordinating political, economic, social and environmental development in the Pacific islands.

A. The growth of urban populations

In most of the larger countries, national populations are increasing at high levels. In Melanesia, the rate of the annual national population growth of Solomon Islands and Vanuatu is higher than 2.8 per cent and in Papua New Guinea it is 2.3 per cent. In Fiji, there has been a slower rate of growth as a consequence of political changes.

In the Polynesian countries, the level of population growth is lower than the rest of the region, owing to the possibility of easy migration from these countries to New Zealand. Niue and Tokalau, being small islands, are experiencing a net decrease in population. The annual population growth rates of Samoa and Tonga are 0.5 and 0.3 per cent respectively. In the Federated States of Micronesia, most states have recorded annual population growth rates close to 2 per cent. However, the Marshall Islands has recorded an annual growth rate of 4.2 per cent. In the context of the broad physical distribution of the population in settlement patterns, the most important feature is that an increasing proportion of the population is living in areas classified as urban.

Among the countries covered in this report, there is no uniform definition of "urban" and different countries apply this classification in the context of their own settlement patterns. A basic criterion is the density of residential settlement and the rate of population growth. In some of the atoll countries, because of the peculiar circumstances of size and lack of land for rural settlement, all rural villages and towns are classed as urban. Nauru classifies all of its population as urban owing to the peculiar nature of the distribution and density of its residential development. On the other hand, Tokalau does not classify any of its population as urban. In the larger countries, all peri-urban areas are classed as urban and in Fiji the "un-incorporated" towns, that is, the small urban centres which do not have an elected local authority, are classified as urban.

Four countries, Cook Islands, the Marshall Islands, Nauru and Palau, now have more than 50 per cent of their population living in urban areas. Cook Islands has a slow rate of population growth owing to emigration. In another five countries, Fiji, Kiribati, Niue, Tonga and Tuvalu, between 30 and 50 per cent of the population is urban. In terms of numbers, Fiji's urbanization is significant in Pacific terms.

Table 1. Urbanization in the South Pacific

	National population (1998 mid-year estimate)	Population density (people/km)	Percentage of urban population	Annual national population growth rate (%)	Annual urban population growth rate (%)	Annual rural population growth rate (%)
Cook Islands	19,200	80	59	0.4	0.5	0.4
Federated States of Micronesia	114,000	159	27	1.9	1.3	2.1
Fiji	785,700	43	46	0.8	2.6	-0.6
Kiribati	85,100	103	37	1.4	2.2	1.0
Marshall Islands	61,000	331	65	4.2	8.2	-0.6
Nauru	11,500	553	100	2.9	2.9	
Niue	2,100	8	32	-1.3	-0.3	-1.6
Palau	18,500	37	71	2.6	3.2	1.3
Papua New Guinea	4,412,400	9	15	2.3	4.1	2.0
Samoa	124,800	58	21	0.5	1.2	0.4
Solomon Islands	417,800	14	13	3.4	6.2	3.1
Tokalau	1,500	125	0	-0.9		-0.9
Tonga	98,000	131	36	0.3	0.7	0.1
Tuvalu	11,000	419	42	1.7	4.8	-0.0
Vanuatu	182,500	15	18	2.8	7.3	2.1

Source: Compiled from secretariat of the Pacific Community, *Pocket Statistical Summary, 1998,* and *Pacific Island Populations,* Wall Chart, 1997, Suva, Fiji.

In Solomon Islands and Vanuatu, the population is largely rural but the urban portion is increasing at more than 6 per cent per annum, one of the highest rates in the world. Some basic information on the relative rates of population growth in the South Pacific is provided in table 1. There is a clear transition from a predominantly rural to a predominantly urban South Pacific region.

An important feature of the pattern of urban growth is that in some countries population is concentrated on the main island. This is a result of the physical nature of the territory and the limited level of economic activities. In Kiribati, some 60 per cent of the national population lives in the Gilbert group, dominated by the main island of South Tarawa. In Samoa, some 70 per cent of the population lives on the island of Upolu (ESCAP 1991).

B. Continuing rural-urban migration

Even though the rural population is relatively large in a number of countries, urbanization and urban living are fast becoming an integral part of the development of the South Pacific nations. The promotion of industrial development, the centralization of the government bureaucracy and the growing service sector all tend to increase urbanization and are likely to focus on capital cities. These processes, which are essential for national economic development, create the forces that encourage rural-urban migration.

The push factors for rural-urban migration include declining commodity prices, continuing high rates of population growth, lack of employment, limited education opportunities and the need to support the wider extended family financially. The pull factors include the monetary economy, prospects for employment in towns, education and lifestyles, recreational and social facilities, changing expectations and the existence of family and clan support networks.

Given the rural base of many national economies in the Pacific, it is natural that rural development programmes will be expanded but their capacity to absorb the increasing workforce and retain it in the rural areas will be limited. Urban populations are increasing through natural increase and rural-urban migration. Moreover, the ongoing transition from subsistence economies to globally integrated cash economies supports the trend towards urbanization.

Primate cities

Pacific capitals are becoming primate cities, being substantially larger than the next largest city, and continue to attract more growth. For example, in Fiji, there is a reasonably well-developed hierarchy of urban centres, but in 1996 metropolitan Suva had four times the population of the second largest city, Lautoka, and is growing three times faster. A feature of metropolitan Suva is that it covers not only the outer-Suva towns of Lami and Nasinu and all the peri-urban development around them but also the town of Nausori, which was once a major centre for sugar production. This town still provides a large rural hinterland with limited services but a large proportion of the population of the town and its suburbs now depends on employment in Suva.

Apia is the only urban centre in Samoa. Similarly, in Solomon Islands, apart from Honiara, there is no substantial urban centre. In Vanuatu, apart from Port Vila and Luganville, there are no urban centres.

In Papua New Guinea, because of the absence of an interconnecting pattern of road links between urban centres, the primacy of Port Moresby is not so marked. The city of Lae has about 40 per cent of the population of Port Moresby, partly because of better road connections with the rich agricultural hinterland. In most of the Federated States of Micronesia, the shortage of land naturally places population growth pressures on the main urban centres.

The increasing pressure for services, employment, housing, schooling and health in many Pacific cities is likely to put a severe strain on national resources in the years to come. Furthermore, people's expectations are rising and standards that proved adequate in the past are less likely to be satisfactory in the future. The information revolution that has enabled most South Pacific countries to access global television networks is increasing the desire for better housing, with a piped water supply and electricity, road access to houses, postsecondary and technical education, better health services and closer access to major national facilities and sporting events. Linked with these desires is the desire for regular paid employment.

C. Urbanization and national economic development

Historically, economic growth and the level of urbanization have been closely related. The physical and social infrastructure provided in urban areas is essential for the development of manufacturing and service industries. Recent World Bank and United Nations studies show that a majority of the national GDP is produced in urban areas (UNCHS 1996a). However, the inefficient provision or absence of essential services such as transportation and communications, security of land tenure, housing, energy, water supply, sewerage and waste management is hindering investment and sound economic development in many countries. Urbanization also enables governments to provide services for social development such as education, health and recreation more efficiently than when the population is spread thinly over the national territory. The positive aspects of urbanization could be fully realized in government planning processes if urbanization is approached in a proactive manner.

D. Physical planning and national economic development planning

Physical planning has had mixed experience in the Pacific. It involves the preparation of plans for the future expansion of an urban or rural settlement through a process of public consultations, based on existing and forecast levels of population and types and directions of physical development. The plan itself depicts, in broad terms, future land use, densities of development, transportation routes and other infrastructure provision, such as water supply and sewerage. It is accompanied by a set of regulations that control development through a process of development approvals. In some regimes it is also accompanied by a programme for investment in infrastructure and other aspects of implementing the plan.

An important feature of the planning process is that landowners must seek planning approval for any development, change of use of the land or the density of occupation, since all such development proposals require the provision of adequate infrastructure and social services by the relevant public authorities.

Some countries in the region have extensive experience, based on the British model of town and country planning, with forward planning, land use zoning schemes, statutory planning, and building and land subdivision bylaws (for example, Fiji, Papua New Guinea and Solomon Islands).

Lack of physical planning

While urban planning has brought about systematic development in parts of some cities, in many others there is limited application in the absence of planning legislation and the necessary institutional framework. The land tenure system, topography, non-availability of services and other factors have tended to create an interrupted pattern of urban development, with areas of undeveloped lands breaking the physical continuity of development.

Apia in Samoa and Nuku'alofa in Tonga, and the cities in the Federated States of Micronesia (except in Kiribati) do not have a legally applicable town plan, even though many plans have been prepared for directing their growth. The local authorities do not have the authority to prepare a legally binding plan for urban expansion and management and the issue is low in the priorities of the relevant central government authorities. This has resulted in uncoordinated and fragmented growth, difficulties in the provision of services, inefficient transport planning, pollution of the lagoon and lack of public spaces.

Box 1. Fiji's successful experience in urban planning

The practice of physical planning in the South Pacific is probably most advanced in Fiji, where the first batch of local authority planning schemes was approved in the early 1960s. Many local authorities have had extensive experience in this area. This includes:

- Preparing a provisional planning scheme, holding public exhibitions and resolving objections and appeals.

- Obtaining legal approval of the planning scheme from the national authority.

- Implementing a process of statutory approvals for all land subdivision, building and other physical development.

- Undergoing a process of revising a planning scheme when the situation so requires.

Over the years, various aspects of environmental management have been incorporated with the land use aspects in the local authority planning schemes. Even though the planning schemes have had the effect of placing limits upon the development wishes of some landowners, they have come to be accepted by the public at large as an essential tool for efficient development of the built environment.

Over the four decades of planning practice in Fiji, the public has seen the benefits through planned improvements in infrastructure and the preservation of sound residential environments. The planning process has also raised the level of awareness among members of the public of the social, economic and environmental effects of different types of urban development and has increased people's capacity to take advantage of the opportunities for public participation in the process of preparing a plan for the future development of their physical environment.

The processes applied now include structure planning linked with investments in infrastructure and social services, as well as development control. The practice of physical planning has also helped to develop the capacity of local governments in the overall process of urban governance.

Source: Personal observations of U. Naiker, fomer General Manager of the National Housing Authority of Fiji.

In Apia, several short-term plans have been prepared but the preparation of long-term development plans has been hindered by the lack of information, lack of town planning expertise, lack of legislation and weak administrative arrangements and concern over the rights of customary landowners. The most recent development plan for Apia was approved by Cabinet in 1992, but its implementation is slow for the reasons stated above (UNCHS 1996b).

Several cities in the Federated States of Micronesia have physical development plans to guide their orderly development but there is a lack of institutional and human resource capacity for implementation. Kiribati introduced the Land Planning Act in 1997, creating the Central Land Planning Board responsible for the preparation of strategic plans. A unique effort is being made in South Tarawa to develop a planning system to suit local institutional and social structures. The Urban Management Plan for South Tarawa has been prepared by the South Tarawa Urban Management Committee through an extensive process of consultations with all landowners and other stakeholders. The consultation process and the workshops held during this planning exercise could serve as a possible model for other countries to consider.

In countries that still have a strong influence of traditional leadership structures in urban management it has been difficult to introduce statutory planning processes. This is partly due to concern on the part of the landowners that they will become subject to control over development of their lands. In such cases, the considerable increase in land values that planning schemes can generate and the potential for such increases to partly finance the investment in infrastructure has not been fully realized.

Linking physical and economic planning

In countries where urban planning has been practised for some time, especially in Melanesia, it has mostly operated without proper linkage with national economic planning. Even though during the formulation of the National Economic Development Plan adequate consultations are made with all departments and other interests within and outside government, the very desirable process of integrating physical planning with economic planning has not been achieved. The result is that certain proposals for economic development cannot proceed efficiently because an adequate physical and social infrastructure is non-existent or insufficient.

Efficient planning and management of urban areas could provide a better base for economic development. Such planning could take into account the standards for land use zoning and the other requirements for planning permission so as to encourage small enterprises and avoid the necessity for unduly heavy investment constraints on new industries that are becoming established. Coordination among various agencies involved in the physical, economic and social issues has been difficult to achieve in spite of the long experience with national economic development planning in some countries.

At the beginning of the decade, the United Nations Development Programme (UNDP) set out very clearly the major thrusts for action in urban management. These are listed in the box 2.

Box 2. UNDP agenda for the 1990s

"To flesh out a people centred approach to urban policy, we have adopted the main points of *Human Development Report 1991*. We focus on the urban problems that represent the most urgent challenges for developing countries during the 1990s. In confronting these problems, it is critical that five issues receive priority attention:

- Alleviate urban poverty by promoting income-generation activities and transforming the role of the informal sector.

- Promote enabling and participatory strategies for the provision of urban infrastructure and affordable shelter.

- Promote the protection and regeneration of the urban physical environment, especially in low-income settlements.

- Improve urban management, including expansion of local governments' revenue-raising capacity and decentralize authority and responsibility for urban development from central government agencies and ministries to local governments and NGOs.

To achieve the above, draw on the full complement of human energy in cities. This means wider recognition of the role of women and full government collaboration with the private and voluntary organizations.

Each of these issues is important in its own right, but all are closely related in allowing developing countries to cope effectively with the transition from rural to urban societies."

Source: *Cities, People and Poverty: Urban Development Cooperation for the 1990s* (UNDP, 1991).

Although the directions outlined by UNDP need to be adapted in the context of small South Pacific island countries, most of them are applicable as they stand, even at the end of this decade.

E. The concept of sustainable human settlements development

Since the early 1990s, there has been considerable discussion of the issue of sustainable development. The report of the Pacific Island developing countries to the United Nations Conference on Environment and Development, held in Rio de Janeiro in 1992, entitled The Pacific Way (SPREP 1992), includes some principles of sustainable development. These include the following:

- To meet the needs of present generations without compromising the ability of future generations to meet their own needs.

- To promote equity in participation in sustainable development.

- To minimize the adverse environmental impacts of economic development through integrating environmental considerations with economic and sectoral planning and policies.

- To formulate resource use and development planning policies which take into account the precautionary principle.

These principles are very relevant to the management of urbanization in the Pacific islands. The concept of sustainable development has become incorporated in Agenda 21, the global plan of action adopted at the Rio Conference, and is being applied increasingly widely at national level and in each country's Agenda 21.

The Global Conference on the Sustainable Development of Small Island Developing States, held in Bridgetown, Barbados, in 1994 translates Agenda 21 into specific policies, actions and measures to be taken at the national, regional and international levels to enable small island developing states to achieve sustainable development (United Nations 1994).

Box 3. Promoting sustainable human settlement development

Paragraph 7.5 of Agenda 21 states that the programme areas included in this field are:

(a)   Providing adequate shelter for all;

(b)   Improving human settlement management;

(c)   Promoting sustainable land-use planning and management;

(d)   Promoting the integrated provision of environmental infrastructure: water, sanitation, drainage and solid-waste management;

(e)   Promoting sustainable energy and transport systems in human settlements;

(f)   Promoting human settlement planning and management in disaster-prone areas;

(g)   Promoting sustainable construction industry activities;

(h)   Promoting human resource development and capacity-building for human settlement development.

Source: Agenda 21: Programme of Action for Sustainable Development (United Nations publication, Sales No. E.93.1.11).

The international movement towards the concept of sustainable development has encouraged other sectors of national and international development to view the issues of sustainability in their particular spheres. In the field of human settlements, the United Nations Centre for Human Settlements (Habitat) (UNCHS) explored the concept in some depth in its preparations for the Rio Conference in the publication entitled *Human Settlements and Sustainable Development* (UNCHS 1990). The concept of sustainable human settlements became enshrined in an international programme through the inclusion of human settlements in Agenda 21, as outlined box 3.

The many socio-economic and environmental problems currently found in cities in the South Pacific make it imperative that efforts are made to define the parameters for sustainable patterns of urban management. The Habitat II conference has elaborated on the various aspects of sustainable human settlements management in an urbanizing world and these, together with recommendations for adequate shelter for all, are contained in the Habitat Agenda (UNCHS 1997a).

This concept of sustainable human settlements development needs to be defined in the specific context of each country for the efficient management of urban and rural centres and for this a regional initiative may be necessary to guide national action. Fiji is currently initiating the legal framework for ensuring sustainable development in urban and rural areas and its experience could be useful to the region.

G. Deteriorating urban living environments

Migration to the major urban centres has been so rapid that national and local governments generally have been unable to provide the necessary services or to set up the systems to enable people to provide some of these services themselves. Most urban migrants live in overcrowded conditions in squatter settlements and slums. These settlements are often located on marginal lands such as stream banks, mangroves, flood-prone areas, hill slopes and lands otherwise unsuitable for development. Central and local governments very seldom provide them with basic infrastructure and services such as roads, water supply, sanitation and solid waste management because the settlements are illegal.

Health issues among the poor have assumed serious proportions owing to certain negative aspects of urbanization. General nutrition levels among the poor are decreasing as opportunities for urban agriculture are limited in the larger cities and traditional food supply systems no longer function.

Overcrowded accommodation in some densely populated atolls (for example, in the Marshall Islands) is leading to respiratory illnesses. Inadequate sanitation causing contamination of shellfish has led to outbreaks of gastrointestinal diseases and hepatitis in Tarawa, Kiribati. The rate of child mortality in the Marshall Islands is one of the highest in the Asian and Pacific region.

In Apia, despite recent improvements, many areas of the city are devoid of drainage. The city characterizes the need for planning and a number of factories and workshops are located in the midst of residential areas. Some areas in the city have dense development of the traditional house ("fales") with very limited open spaces around them. Thus, improvement in planning in Apia has become a prime issue that needs to be dealt with immediately, in order to preserve the quality of life (UNCHS 1996b).

H. Increasing social problems

Various institutional, cultural and social factors affect the nature and pace of the adaptation from village to town living. The national development process in the Pacific involves the movement of people on a scale unprecedented in traditional societies.

In urban areas there is considerable strain on the traditional social value systems developed over centuries. These traditional leadership structures continue to serve well in the rural areas but in the urban settlements family and clan-based authority systems are breaking down. The social disruption caused by the division of families between urban and rural areas and the loss of traditional "safety nets" has contributed to higher levels of divorce, single parent families and a rise in domestic violence. Insecurity and rapid urban growth have caused tensions between migrant groups, landowners and urban authorities.

Unemployment is one of the major problems associated with urbanization in the South Pacific. Many employment policies and programmes stress formal sector jobs instead of improvements in the subsistence or informal sectors. The growth potential in the small business sector remains undeveloped. In Port Moresby, up to one third of the urban population is seeking work and in other urban centres of Papua New Guinea unemployment is more than 10 per cent. The numbers of the unemployed are rising as new batches of the younger generation join the workforce (Connell, 1999). Unfulfilled expectations of the urban settlers have spawned alcohol and drug abuse, family violence and -- what has become the most publicized social problem in Papua New Guinea -- criminal youth gangs (UNCHS 1993). Unemployment is also one of the causes of the rising incidence of crime in the large cities. In Port Moresby, some 69 per cent of the unemployed men are known to be living through crime (Connell, 1999).

The concentration of people in urban areas has greatly improved the economics of the informal sector and in many towns micro and small businesses are thriving. The informal sector takes different forms in different countries. In the smaller countries, informal jobs include bottle collecting, street vending, newspaper selling, car washing, shoe polishing. In the larger countries in the region, many of the building trades, vehicle repairs and a whole range of activities are undertaken in the informal sector.

This is an important sector of the urban economy as high population growth, young population structure, relatively slow economic growth rates and very limited potential for labour absorption in the formal sectors imply that, for island countries, absorption of the unemployed will critically rely upon the small businesses and micro-enterprises which operate in the informal sector. However, the informal sector operates under many constraints which arise from central and local government legislation and administrative procedures.

Poverty

The South Pacific islands enjoy a reasonable level of subsistence income in the rural areas but in urban areas the cash economy has become dominant. Over the last decade, almost all countries have witnessed low or stagnant economic growth while the population has continued to grow. In a number of countries, the available financial resources have had to be diverted to cyclone-related rehabilitation and humanitarian relief efforts. The effects of the slow rate of economic growth are felt most in urban areas and are a constraint on improving the standard of living and advancing human development.

In recent years, several countries have restructured a number of government institutions through a process of commercialization, corporatization or privatization. In some services this has resulted in the removal of subsidies, with the consequent adverse effect on the poor. A 1997 Fiji poverty study showed that one in four households could not afford a basic standard of living, with a majority of the poor living in urban areas (Government of Fiji and UNDP 1997).

Human development index

UNDP has explored the concept of sustainable human development, which seeks to refocus attention on the ultimate objective of development, increasing the opportunities for people to lead productive and satisfying lives. This implies assessing development in terms of a range of social and economic indicators and not just in terms of income growth (UNDP 1994). This approach is captured in the concept of human development which is assessed by UNDP through the compilation of the human development index (HDI) for each country. The human development index was first published in 1991 in the Human Development Report. The index is based on a range of socio-economic indicators such as life expectancy at birth, child mortality, adult literacy, access to safe water and health services, employment and wages and the status of women. A global ranking is undertaken based on the index. Table 2 shows some of the key indicators and the human development index for the countries of the South Pacific in 1998.

Table 2. Human development index for Pacific island countries, 1998

Country	Adult literacy (per cent)	Combined gross enrolment (per cent)	Life expectancy at birth	GDP per capita (US $)	HDI	Global HDI rank[a]
Palau	91.4	83.4	69.0	8,027	0.861	46
Cook Islands	93.2	84.8	72.0	4,947	0.822	62
Niue	97.0	83.6	74.0	3,714	0.744	70
Fiji	92.9	81.3	66.5	2,684	0.667	101
Nauru	95.0	79.5	58.2	3,450	0.663	103
Tonga	99.0	83.3	68.0	1,868	0.647	107
Samoa	95.7	85.7	66.6	1,060	0.590	117
Tuvalu	95.0	74.0	67.0	1,157	0.583	118
Federated States of Micronesia	71.3	71.4	65.7	2,070	0.569	120
Marshall Islands	74.4	71.7	65.0	1,182	0.563	121
Kiribati	92.2	67.8	61.6	702	0.515	129
Vanuatu	33.5	57.4	65.8	1,231	0.425	140
Solomon Islands	30.3	34.8	64.7	926	0.371	147
Papua New Guinea	28.2	28.6	54.0	1,196	0.314	164
Tokelau	91.0	88.3	69.0	n.a.	n.a.	n.a.

Source: *Pacific Human Development Report 1999* (UNDP, Suva, 1999)

[a] Ranking is applied according to the 1998 Human Development Report.

II. URBAN INFRASTRUCTURE

Governments are making continuous efforts to improve infrastructure. The advent of cars, higher levels of consumption and changing lifestyles require improved levels of infrastructure. However, infrastructure for urban development such as roads, water supply, sewerage, solid waste disposal, electricity and communications is failing to keep up with the needs of the growing urban populations.

The installation of infrastructure requires considerable investment, and this is beyond the reach of most countries in the region. As well as insufficient financial resources, a number of local management issues hinder large-scale investment. These include the limited capacity for maintenance of the existing plant and, in some countries, a reluctance to adopt user-pay policies that would create possibilities for sound financial management of the investment.

A. Water supply

Most countries in the South Pacific are well endowed with water but the level of water consumption is gradually rising in some countries, while in others there is over-consumption. In Samoa, for example, in some instances consumption levels have reached 600-700 litres per capita per day, compared to the WHO accepted average of 250 litres per capita per day. This is mainly due to uncontrolled use, waste and leaks in the network (UNCHS 1996b). The importance of conserving water resources is not fully appreciated in parts of the region where the water supply is free.

Some of the important issues of urban water supply systems in the region are given below:

- Reservoir capacities need to be improved in many towns to meet the growing needs of urban settlements.

- Water resources are limited in the atoll towns where water lenses are often polluted, for example in Kiribati and Tuvalu.

- Droughts affect parts of the larger islands of Melanesia, as well as some of the atoll countries.

- Salt-water intrusion into freshwater lenses due to sea level rise is a possible threat to coastal water resources.

In some countries, there is mismanagement of water supply systems as evidenced by leakage because of lack of maintenance, inefficient billing and poor collection of charges. Attempts to meter the water supply have often met with protests from local populations who believe that water is nature's gift to humans and hence that they should not have to pay for it (UNCHS 1996b).

B. Sewerage

A very small proportion of the Pacific urban population has satisfactory sewage services. There are few sewage treatment plants and their coverage is limited, mainly because of the relatively large scale of investment necessary, both for the headworks and for the reticulation system. For the latter, the process of acquiring right of way for sewer lines over private properties, leased lands and unleased lands under customary tenure is cumbersome and time-consuming. In Fiji, with its long history of urban management, only 25 per cent of the population of metropolitan Suva is connected to the sewerage system (UNCHS 1992). In

Papua New Guinea, only about 11 per cent of the urban population has a piped sewerage system (Connell and Lea 1993). The few successful on-site treatment solutions only operate on a small scale.

Many places use ocean outfalls for sewage disposal (Honiara, South Tarawa and Kiribati). The risks of foreshore contamination are high, with negative effects on marine resources and eventual leaching back into the freshwater lens. The lagoons beside Fanga'uta in Tonga, Port Vila, Suva and Tarawa have sufficiently high fecal coliform levels to be a public health concern.

The lack of reticulated sewerage systems has resulted in a proliferation of septic tanks and, in some cities, of pit latrines as well. In Suva, surface pollution from septic tanks in the non-sewered suburbs and pit latrines in squatter settlements causes serious public health problems. In other cities, even where soil conditions are suitable, during the rainy season septic tanks tend to overflow, causing serious health concerns in low-lying areas. In the Marshall Islands, surface pollution from septic tanks, pit latrines, and household and domestic waste contaminating the underlying water lenses is widespread.

Overall, the inadequate disposal of human waste is one of the serious environmental problems in the Pacific.

C. Solid waste management

The amount of disposable solid waste is increasing as lifestyles and consumption patterns in the Pacific change to western ways, with increasing levels of non-biodegradable materials such as cans, bottles and plastics. There are very few programmes for solid waste reduction. The practice of recycling waste, such as bottle collecting, is undertaken only at a basic level. The technology required for establishing appropriate facilities for waste recycling of paper, cans and plastics is beyond the capacity of most Pacific island countries. In some cases, the volume of waste cannot be economically recycled. The usual methods of disposal are landfills, dumping on seashores, estuaries, swamps and mangroves, often resulting in polluted waterways, lagoons and water supply.

In many urban centres, even in the larger countries, suitable sites for the disposal of domestic solid waste have been difficult to obtain. In Suva, after several years of negotiations with landowners, a new disposal site just outside the city boundary, between the seashore and the main road, has replaced the existing landfill site. In Nadi, Fiji, the town council has been unable to identify a suitable site on account of the flood-prone nature of the surrounding areas and proximity to the international airport. It has come to an arrangement to use the landfill site of the neighbouring Lautoka City Council. However, this site on Crown land has been subject to regular roadblocks mounted by the native owners of adjacent lands as the public access to the site traverses customary land.

In the atoll countries, the sheer non-availability of land for disposal of solid waste is serious, as witnessed in Funafuti, Tuvalu. Community attitudes to disposal of wastes have not changed to match the nature and volume of waste that need to be managed. In the allocation of lands for different uses, solid waste disposal is a very low priority. The disposal of industrial wastes containing dangerous and illegal pollutants will become an issue as the level of industrialization increases.

D. Infrastructure financing

Investment in urban infrastructure such as major roads, water supply and sanitation is usually financed from central government resources. In most urban centres there are severe backlogs in the expansion of existing systems and to serve new urban growth. Maintenance of the existing facilities often lags owing to lack of planning and finance and the shortage of skills. In some cases, there is inefficient use of financial resources caused by institutional problems that prevent public funds from reaching the beneficiaries who need them most. In several countries, cost recovery on services provided is limited. Wherever costs of services are charged, the richer suburbs pay the same rate as the poor ones. With the poor economic performance of most countries, there is very little or no budgetary provision for expansion of infrastructure. Financial institutions like national development banks have low capacity. The World Bank and the Asian Development Bank have assessed the extent of the investment required for improving urban infrastructure in a number of cities and sound infrastructure management practices could facilitate the inflow of funds.

E. Environmental management

Urban areas in the Pacific countries face a number of environmental dangers. These include:

- A precarious balance between population growth and land capacity, with population densities in some localized areas being very significant.

- Pollution of rivers and lagoons through indiscriminate waste disposal.

- An expected rise in the sea level.

- Strain on the coastal ecology from the large numbers of urban settlements located in coastal zones.

- Disaster mitigation against cyclones, earthquakes, floods and droughts.

Environmental management is a distinct programme area in regional and national development and the South Pacific Regional Environmental Programme (SPREP) has assisted in developing national environmental protection legislation in many countries. Most countries already have national environmental management strategies and are attempting to gradually increase their institutional and human resource capacities for applying environmental management practices.

III. HOUSING

Throughout the Pacific, rural areas do not have a serious housing problem. The availability of secure land with a basic level of services, usually at no cost, easy access to appropriate building materials, community-based construction efforts and a limited need for finance together ensure that all households have adequate housing. However, in urban areas these basic housing inputs either do not exist or are unaffordable, especially for the middle and lower income sectors of the urban population. The formal housing market caters largely to the upper income groups because of the cost and access to long-term loans. Those without access to affordable housing are left to their own initiative and various ad hoc solutions are devised in the context of the prevailing land tenure and socio-economic situations.

A. International initiatives

The inability of the urban poor to access adequate housing is a universal trend and considerable efforts have been made at the global level by the United Nations and the World Bank through programmes such as sites and services and settlements upgrading, to ensure adequate and affordable housing for the poor. In the last two decades, the United Nations Centre for Human Settlements (UNCHS) has undertaken a series of initiatives to encourage governments to improve national housing policies.

The International Year of Shelter for the Homeless (IYSH), observed in 1987 and for which UNCHS was the organizing secretariat, marked a major change in the commitment of the global community to improve national housing policies. The programme for IYSH identified a number of innovative solutions in different countries to provide adequate shelter for the poor. The IYSH South Pacific regional workshop reviewed many of the key issues and prepared a series of recommendations for action to improve housing (Papua New Guinea University of Technology 1985).

The global momentum generated in the search for affordable housing for the poor resulted in the adoption by the General Assembly of the Global Strategy for Shelter to the Year 2000 (UNCHS 1988). This programme focused on "enabling strategies" whereby governments were to be facilitators, enabling the deployment of the resources of the private, household and community sectors.

A further development for assisting governments in improving their national housing policies was the development of the urban and housing indicators by UNCHS and the World Bank. The application of these has enabled all stakeholders to identify aspects of housing policy that acted as constraints to access to affordable housing. In the South Pacific these were thoroughly considered at the Global Shelter Strategy South Pacific Sub-regional seminar, held in Brisbane in 1993 (University of Queensland 1993).

These international and regional initiatives have assisted many governments to address constraints to the orderly operation of markets in the housing sector. The focus of international initiatives has been on formulating enabling strategies, with governments concentrating on establishing the institutional and legal frameworks for land supply, planning, infrastructure and housing finance, leaving it to people's initiatives through the operations of the private sector, community and cooperative organizations and household efforts to seek housing solutions.

Many examples throughout the developing countries indicate that people, with only limited official assistance, build better and cheaper houses than government agencies. Many squatter and informal settlements have been transformed into regular suburbs over time, given the support of central and local governments to supplement people's initiatives.

B Housing policy responses in the South Pacific

In the Pacific almost all governments have taken initiatives to address the housing problems of the needy in urban areas. In the absence of a viable private sector market, the official responses have been varied and have gradually changed over time.

The Fiji Housing Authority and the Papua New Guinea National Housing Corporation have accumulated extensive experience over three decades and have come up with a range of solutions. Their programmes provide a choice of housing solutions for different levels of affordability and preference. Serviced sites are provided for people to undertake self-building. The actual building operations can be undertaken on a self-help basis by engaging specialist trades people such as plumbers and electricians or by letting out a contract to a small-time builder. Other choices include complete houses or core houses for purchase, houses or flats for rental at subsidized rates, serviced sites and cash loans for self-building, settlements upgrading and village and rural housing.

A variety of factors have constrained their output, in particular the non-availability of a regular supply of land for development and the high initial standards for infrastructure required by the approving authorities, which place their products beyond the financial reach of many in need of affordable housing. The subsidies on the rental housing schemes could not be sustained for long and the reforms introduced during the 1990s in all Pacific island countries focus on the financial sustainability of public housing programmes.

The Papua New Guinea National Housing Corporation's new policies are to develop serviced plots for leasing on a self-financing basis, to sell the existing housing stock while increasing rents on the remaining houses to market levels, and to leave rental housing construction to the private sector (UNCHS 1993).

In Fiji, the rental housing programme was initiated for the very poor who were not eligible for other housing solutions because of the levels of their income. They paid around 15 per cent of their income as rent but since the rental subsidy could not be absorbed into the financial restructuring of the Housing Authority the public housing rental programme was transferred to a newly created Public Rental Board. This body does not have the financial capacity to undertake a building programme to respond to the need. Consequently, the urban poor have a serious housing problem and church groups have taken some initiatives to provide housing solutions for the poor.

Other countries have limited experience in institutional responses to the housing need. The Kiribati Housing Corporation caters only for civil servants. The Samoa Housing Corporation is a financing organization. In Solomon Islands, the Housing Authority was disbanded after some years and settlements with basic standards were developed on sites designated as "traditional housing areas". In Vanuatu, the Housing Corporation, established in 1985, is trying to address serious problems with very limited capacity.

C. Housing markets

The demand for affordable housing is increasing as a result of the growing urban populations. The demand comes from new household formation within the existing population and from new migrants. Existing houses are constantly being upgraded. In almost every country, except possibly Nauru, housing market mechanisms are not functioning due to constraints on the development of customary lands and the absence of financial mechanisms that meet different affordability levels. The absence of security of tenure, which normally provides collateral or security for a housing loan, inhibits the development of housing finance mechanisms.

As a result of these factors, the private sector plays a limited role in housing. The limited housing stock commands high prices for purchase or rent. The building industry is therefore unable to play its usual role as a generator of economic growth and creator of employment opportunities. Additionally, those small businesses and micro-enterprises that are dependent on the building industry are unable to contribute to alleviating unemployment.

Towns in Papua New Guinea have inherited the colonial tradition of employer- provided rental housing. Thus, there is only a very small private housing market, mainly for expatriates, and no tradition of home ownership. Moreover, both the government (the major employer) and private enterprises want to rid themselves of the costly role of employee housing provision. Those urban residents who do not have an employer willing to provide formal sector housing must either depend on relatives who do have houses or turn to informal self-help, which usually means squatter settlements (UNCHS 1993).

In Cook Islands and Niue, a growing number of houses have been abandoned by the owners who have emigrated. The houses are left in a state of disrepair but the house cannot be sold to interested parties owing to the complexities of the customary ownership system.

Building materials

Except for the atoll islands, most of the region has adequate timber products. However, many other types of building materials are required to meet the growing expectations of urban dwellers. The size of the market, even in Fiji and Papua New Guinea, is insufficient for the level of investment required for local production of a wide range of building materials. Thus, an important feature of the building industry in the South Pacific is the high amount of importation, particularly from Australia and New Zealand to Melanesia and Polynesia, and from the United States of America to the Federated States of Micronesia. In the Marshall Islands, maintenance of the housing stock is becoming a serious issue.

In Papua New Guinea, the construction industry still operates in an environment inherited from colonial days. This results in excessive dependence on large construction companies, imported building materials, and construction methods developed for high-wage and high-technology societies. This situation results in a very large gap between traditional methods and materials and formal sector methods and materials (UNCHS 1993).

A particular aspect of residential buildings is cyclone-resistant design and construction. Despite the many advantages of traditional design of roofs and superstructure, there is a strong desire for building houses to modern western designs and using modern materials.

D. Housing finance capacity

Housing finance systems, managed by public sector institutions, already exist in several countries and the prospects of expanding their capacities are improving as national provident funds mobilize more savings. Commercial banks and insurance companies could also play a role in mobilizing capital for housing and there is potential for community-based saving schemes.

However, most formal sector financing systems require loan security and thus the land tenure system plays a crucial role. The legislation and procedures for mortgage lending have to be well established in order to enable a housing finance system to function.

In Fiji, where the housing finance system is well developed, the Fiji National Provident Fund serves as the main provider of investment funds and the Housing Authority as the provider of loans for the middle income sector. The Home Finance Company, which serves the higher income market, is more closely linked with commercial financial markets and mobilizes capital for housing loans from these sources.

In the absence of security of tenure for mortgage financing, alternate approaches need to be devised. In Fiji, many village housing schemes undertaken on lands that cannot be leased or mortgaged are backed by legally accepted guarantees from appropriately resourced persons or bodies. The Samoa Housing Corporation, which functions mainly as a housing finance institution, accepts assurances from senior clan members as security for housing loans.

Overseas examples of community financing need to be studied for their adaptation in the South Pacific urban culture. The Grameen Bank, a private initiative, has provided loans to a large number of rural poor in Bangladesh on the basis of community loan guarantees. A small group of successful past borrowers provides guarantees for repayment by the borrower and the loan repayment levels achieved are higher than those of commercial banks. The Urban Community Development Office of the Government of Thailand operates as an independent programme out of the National Housing Authority. Seed funding and loans to community-based savings and credit schemes are provided for a range of community improvement activities, among which housing is predominant.

E. Informal settlements

High construction costs, resulting from the high cost of imported building materials, costly building regulations and high urban wages add to affordability problems for the poor seeking adequate shelter. The experience of the Fiji Housing Authority over the past 30 years shows that some 70 per cent of the applicants for housing are unable to afford the repayments for the purchase of low-cost houses, which conform to legal requirements. The poor are left to find solutions in overcrowded accommodation or as squatters. The result is the haphazard growth of informal settlements on unsuitable sites and on the urban fringes of most large cities in the region. In these types of settlements, the settlers make arrangements with the landowners to occupy a building site on affordable terms but without security of tenure. Hence, there is no incentive for making permanent investment in housing, and corrugated iron shacks are the standard form of construction. People tend to expand houses incrementally, adding and improving according to the increasing needs of the growing family. A whole new generation of young people is growing up in these settlements throughout the South Pacific.

In most of the larger cities there are many pockets of such informal housing developments with very limited or no infrastructure and services. In Suva, there are 26 squatter settlements within the city boundaries (UNCHS 1992). In Papua New Guinea, squatter settlements housing up to 50 per cent of the population have developed around Port Moresby, Lae, Mount Hagen and Rabaul (UNCHS 1993). Relatively large settlements also exist at Blacksands and Federation in Port Vila, Vanuatu. If this trend remains unchecked, it will result in a serious deterioration of the living environment and will pose a serious danger to public health.

Eviction

Informal settlements are of different types. They range from pure squatters on state lands to quasi-legal renting of customary lands. Squatters on state lands are illegal occupiers of the land. On customary lands, there is often proper negotiation with the leadership of the landowning clan. The construction of houses takes place with the explicit or implied consent of the landowner. Sometimes, there are middlemen operating either on behalf of the landowners or on behalf of a particular needy group. The arrangements made are insecure and lead to misunderstandings.

The removal of settlers is sometimes necessary to enable public utility works to be undertaken. Wherever this happens on state-owned land, adequate compensation and resettlement arrangements are made. There have been cases where the owners of customary land have evicted settlers born on their lands in urban areas. In such cases, no resettlement arrangements are made. Some past cases of evictions, for example in Lae, have resulted in major calamity for the urban poor. The irony is that evicted squatters have to go and settle elsewhere. In most such cases the local, provincial or national governments have been unable to offer permanent solutions.

A more sympathetic view of informal settlements is gradually emerging. This is arising from a number of developments, which include the following:

- Greater realization that the efforts of the poor in constructing houses in informal settlements represent an economic and social investment and that the bulk of the savings of the poor are directed to housing.

- The settlers usually build up strong community relationships as these settlements represent a mingling of people from different parts of the country.

- Greater awareness of projects where squatters have improved their living environments after acquiring security of tenure.

- Increasing pressure on national governments from international organizations such as UNDP, UNCHS and the World Bank for upgrading informal settlements, introducing enabling strategies and alleviating poverty.

- The growing movement on the right to adequate housing promoted by the Centre for Human Rights and major international NGOs such as the Habitat International Coalition.

The whole scenario of eviction is a symptom of the failure of governments to appreciate the dynamics at play in the economic development and urbanization processes. Land is recognized by economists as a basic ingredient of economic growth and the failure of housing is largely a failure by governments to ensure affordable and secure access to land. The need to resettle people can be avoided by a proactive programme of sites provision. However, where there is need for resettlement, the process needs to conform to sound principles.

Box 4. Essentials of good resettlement planning

1. Fair and equitable compensation for lost assets, livelihoods and incomes.

2. Restoration (or enhancement) of living standards and livelihoods through housing replacement and income restoration programmes.

3. Adoption of participatory planning strategies.

4. Dealing with the special problems of vulnerable groups in society.

Source: Asian Development Bank, "Resettlement policy and practice in South-East Asia and the Pacific: proceedings of workshops held in Manila and Port Vila, 1998" (revised draft, January 1999)

The Asian Development Bank, in recognition of the need for some guiding principles, organized two workshops on the subject, one of them specifically for the Pacific island countries. These principles are shown in the box 4.

Settlement upgrading

Settlement upgrading has become a common practice in many developing countries. Wherever the land occupied in informal settlements is not required for an essential public purpose, tenure is granted to squatters and infrastructure and services are upgraded. The major features of such programmes are:

- Community involvement in the planning and execution of the upgrading project.

- Improved security of tenure for the residents.

- Improved infrastructure services such as vehicular and footpath access, water supply, sewerage, drainage and electricity supply.

- Provision of social facilities such as kindergartens or schools, health facilities, religious and community buildings.

- Opportunities for income generation through the establishment of market buildings.

Perhaps the most well known example of a large-scale national settlement upgrading programme is the Kampung Improvement Programme of Indonesia. This programme has improved the living conditions in thousands of informal urban and rural settlements throughout the country.

In the South Pacific region, an example of a large-scale housing project that involved a considerable amount of settlement upgrading and squatter resettlement is the Vitogo and Drasa scheme at Lautoka in Fiji undertaken by the Housing Authority. These two programmes are described in box 5, based upon information from internal files and progress reports of the Housing Authority.

Box 5. Vitogo and Drasa resettlement scheme, Lautoka, Fiji

This scheme is on about 300 hectares of peri-urban land located just outside the Lautoka town boundary. The land was freehold, owned by the sugar company, which had allowed its employees to build their homes on sites allotted on the basis of an annual tenancy. Plots were not surveyed but were numbered on plans. Over the decades many sugar mill employees and their offspring built their houses and the area attracted a steady stream of squatters in spite of controls. Very few houses were built with permanent building materials.

There was a minimum of vehicular access, a haphazard system of water supply and electricity supply, no sewerage provision, no security of tenure for community buildings such as schools, temples, mosques, churches and public halls. Over a thousand households resided on the usable portion of the land. About a third of the area was steep and not easy to occupy. As part of the overall rationalization of the sugar industry, around 1970, the sugar company transferred the land to the government, which leased it to the Fiji Housing Authority for orderly residential and related development.

In compliance with the Lautoka town planning scheme, an overall upgrading proposal of the whole area was prepared showing the different residential zones, the location of all new minor and major roads, water supply and sewerage provisions, shopping centres, sites for schools and religious buildings, parks, etc.

Negotiations were concluded with the Lautoka City Council for relaxing some of the standards applying to infrastructure so as to increase the affordability of serviced sites for the maximum number of households. A 10-year development scheme was prepared for investment, together with costing and pricing of the developed sites. The detailed plans accompanying the scheme showed the effect on each existing tenancy, house, crops and any site improvements. The plan was executed in stages after a considerable amount of community consultation. The major characteristics of the scheme were:

Box 5. (continued)

The preservation of the maximum number of existing house sites and minimal dislocation of existing houses to make way for public uses.

An agreed formula for compensation for house relocation, damage to valuable trees.

Residents who were not eligible for the cheapest site were offered subsidized rental accommodation.

Cross-subsidy for lower income groups through the differential pricing of higher class residential leases, some of which were allocated through a tendering process.

Allocation of a 99-year sublease over subdivided house sites to existing tenants and their offspring resident in the area but without a house.

Replacement of the old labour lines associated with the sugar mill.

Employment opportunities for local residents in the land development works. An agreement to allow the Housing Authority to undertake its housing programmes on any unallocated land.

Source: Fiji Housing Authority internal files and project progress reports.

IV. LAND SUPPLY AND DEMAND

Land is an essential component in the urbanization process. The increasing population in the cities requires new areas for housing, schools, recreation areas and religious buildings. Where suitable, affordable and secure sites are not available, these needs are met by informal or illegal means. The pace of urbanization is such that new attitudes and approaches to land development in urban areas are necessary in almost every Pacific island country.

Land supply constraints are at the heart of many problems of sound urban management in the Pacific. As noted above, there is a clear linkage between security of tenure, the development of housing finance systems and the performance of the building industry. Security of tenure is thus directly linked to prospects for employment generation and income-earning capacity and therefore to poverty alleviation.

However, in all the countries in the region, the land market does not function normally since a large section of national land assets does not enter the urban land market. Approximately 80 per cent of land in the Pacific islands is under some form of customary land tenure, which is governed by a range of policies and practices that constrain national development.

A. Customary lands

The customary land tenure system is based on ownership of lands by indigenous families or social groupings. The diverse tenure systems in the Pacific were devised for subsistence agriculture, in situations where people produced almost all their own food (Crocombe 1989). The systems were flexible and catered adequately for changing needs in a rural setting. After the advent of colonialism, western systems of rigid rights were introduced.

In most countries, a certain portion of the land was alienated soon after contact with Europeans and this practice was stopped by legislation. In some countries, there are restrictions on the allocation of customary lands under leases. Land has a special significance for the people but, in urban areas, there is now a conflict between traditional views and the modern needs of urban development. A major issue is the need to adapt tenure systems to populations up to 10 times higher than they were at the time of first contact with European cultures, and these populations are concentrated in towns and other non-traditional centres and earn their living from non-subsistence activities (Crocombe 1994).

B. Demand for land

Land supply is failing to keep up with the demands of urbanization in almost all countries. Land is generally not available for most aspects of urban development, including infrastructure, industrial estates, housing, social facilities and recreational needs.

A number of countries have freehold land but the amount is very limited and most of it is developed as these parcels are located in or near urban settlements. Most countries also have state land, known as Crown land in some countries. This is also largely developed, in urban as well as rural areas.

Scope is limited for increasing land through reclamation in lagoons owing to the well-documented negative impacts on the ecology, including food sources, and therefore on nutrition and health. Land shortage is serious in some of the atoll countries and land reclamation is being undertaken in a number of urban centres in the Federated States of

Micronesia. In Kiribati, land is so scarce that reclamation of lagoons is seen as a way of providing the government with new sites for various uses.

Governments in some countries have been unable to negotiate with the landowners for the use of land for public purposes. Some have shown a lack of political will to exercise eminent domain powers for compulsory land acquisition for public purposes even though the necessary legislation exists.

In Papua New Guinea, where some 95 to 97 per cent of the land is under customary ownership, these lands cannot be sold outright or mortgaged, effectively disqualifying the use of the land as collateral for loans and reducing incentives to conserve land. Almost none of the land is surveyed or registered, so disputes are usually settled through violent feuds rather than courts of law. With rising demographic pressures, land disputes have become more common (UNCHS 1993). The customary land tenure system is complex due to the different levels of decision-making and the varying interests of the different owners of a particular parcel of land. In some countries, customary land may not be made available to people outside the clan of the owners.

In Fiji, the administration and development of native lands is the responsibility of the Native Lands Trust Board (NLTB). The Board obtains consent from the landowners, subdivides the land and leases the new plots to meet the demand. It administers several thousand leases for all types of urban and rural uses.

NLTB has been in operation for about 50 years and retains around 25 per cent of the rent income to defray its administration costs. The remainder of the rent is distributed to the landowners and their chiefs. Because it operates as a trustee organization, NLTB has not been able to set aside a development fund. Similarly, the landowners have not been able to allocate some of the regular rent income towards a development fund. Sometimes, customary lands can be obtained for urban uses through ad hoc arrangements with the land owners without the involvement of NLTB, but the insecurity of tenure discourages entrepreneurship and investment by the tenant, as is witnessed in the peri-urban settlements in Fiji.

In Papua New Guinea, in recognition of the future need to utilize customary land for development purposes, the government developed the Land Mobilization Programme in 1989, aimed in part at urban areas. However, success has been slow. It has become common for land tenure to be secured through private agreements with the customary owners rather than the official process of government registration and lease title (UNCHS 1993). In Vanuatu, some bold measures were taken by declaring public ownership over urban land. Matters concerning the allocation of rental income to the original native owners and legal contests against declaration of public ownership over customary lands in the urban area are being resolved. In the Marshall Islands, there is no public land and coastal erosion is being caused by the extraction of sand and rock.

C. Land subdivision standards

The supply of land for urban uses involves more than mere availability. A minimum level of infrastructure in terms of access roads and water supply is essential for settlement at urban densities.

A combination of central and local government regulations and procedures set high standards for land surveying and the installation of infrastructure for creating smaller parcels or subdividing land for urban settlement. Complying with the high standards results in unaffordable costs even to middle income groups. The standards are set high partly because local government bodies do not have the capital resources to upgrade the infrastructure later.

This is a problem facing many urban centres and needs to be resolved to activate the formal land market.

Solomon Islands has addressed the issue of standards by creating "traditional housing areas". These have gravelled roads, open drains, no sewerage system and a shared water supply. This has enabled people to settle within their affordability limits.

D. Constraints on the development of customary land

Land rights are an integral part of the Pacific cultural and social systems and a number of factors constrain an orderly land supply to meet the demands of urban growth. These include the following:

- Customary landowners are not culturally disposed to alienating land and have a tendency to retain full control of their land in case future generations have need of it.

- The procedures for leasing and development of customary land are either not well developed or are very complex and time-consuming.

- Those customary landowners who have responded to the demand find difficulties in meeting the high land subdivision standards and the cost of basic infrastructure in order to provide potential tenants with security of tenure.

- The system does not encourage capital accumulation for land development.

- Rent income is spread out. The owners are therefore unable to take advantage of the growing demand for urban land.

E. Land titling

Only a few countries have adequate cadastres showing land parcels, ownership, rights and easements over land, charges and encumbrances. Land mapping and titling is incomplete in many countries, and this creates considerable delays in the resolution of disputes over boundaries, ownership and user rights. There are many advantages in having good records but the process of establishing a system is long and costly.

In Samoa and some areas in the Federated States of Micronesia, land titling projects have been initiated but, owing to lack of adequate resources, little progress has been made. Modern electronic technologies can speed up the mapping process and facilitate these procedures but the process of clearly settling conflicting claims needs to be undertaken through adjudication.

Fiji has benefited from continuous advances in mapping and aerial photography of the national territory and the use of electronic land information systems for various aspects of land management. It also maintains the position of Commissioner for Native Lands for the resolution of disputes concerning native lands and associated rights.

Many countries have established a geographical information system (GIS) unit in land management agencies. This has simplified certain procedures but the full potential of GIS has not been realized. The technology requires constant upgrading of skills, as well as computer hardware and software.

V. COMMUNITY PARTICIPATION AND HUMAN RESOURCES

Urbanization poses new problems, as well as opportunities for the involvement of people in resolving problems at a scale never encountered in the rural areas. Urban areas comprise a rich mixture of people from different parts of the country, with different approaches to the resolution of problems. They all have the common goal of improving their quality of life and it is a challenge for central and local governments to channel all public and community initiatives towards this goal.

The global trend is for greater public participation in decision-making for urban management through public consultations, urban and civic forums and similar organized groupings. Through the information revolution, people are more aware of what is achievable to meet their rising expectations. Thus, appropriate mechanisms are necessary at the central and city levels to enable people to articulate their needs and to contribute to solutions.

A. Community participation

The people are a major resource in the Pacific and this resource needs to be fully utilized. In the rural areas and villages, participation of communities, under the traditional leadership structures, is quite common and effective in decision-making for local development.

However, in urban areas, the social cohesion of the rural areas is no longer present and therefore opportunities for community participation are rare. As problems in urban management can be quite complex and often concern the interests of particular groups, the involvement of communities can help to resolve complicated issues.

In all consideration of public participation it is important to distinguish between participation with labour or sweat equity in a project requiring physical effort and participation in which the participants are fully involved in the process of policy formulation, affecting the local environment, including the raising of sensitive issues. There are many examples of the former but not many of the latter.

B. Urban and civic forums

Urban summits, along the lines of the national summits being used widely in the Pacific, could be organized for all stakeholders in a particular urban area or on a specific issue to consider options and select lines of action to seek solutions. The stakeholders include settlers, landowners, local authorities, government agencies, NGOs, community associations, academics, the business sector and religious organizations. Urban forums have become a useful vehicle for public participation in many Asian cities.

C. Non-governmental organizations

Non-governmental organizations working in housing, infrastructure and services are active in many countries, acting either individually or as national networks. Their actions range over many aspects of human development and include the following:

- Working with and for disadvantaged people such as children, women, refugees, the indigenous, elderly, poor, hungry, disabled, and disaster victims.

- Addressing disadvantage through projects and programmes such as welfare services, education, skills training, income generation, housing, credit and financial services, food production, and small-scale manufacturing.

- Raising awareness through information and communication, research and training, campaigning and advocacy, networking and collective action.

- Taking action on issues detrimental to the well-being of people or society such as peace, human rights, the environment, gender issues, and economic structural adjustment.

Among the more prominent NGOs active in the region are the Urban Shelter Network of Lae, HART (Housing Assistance and Relief Trust) and the Methodist Church in Fiji, the Samoan church groups that provide housing for rural migrants and some cooperative societies. Their work is often hampered by legal and procedural constraints and they require support from national and local governments in many small ways to enable them to deliver assistance to those in need.

D. Private sector

The real estate industry has a limited role in land development and housing in the region owing to the limited availability of land for urban development. The private sector has been active in the building and infrastructure construction and transportation areas but not in the management of services such as water supply. Although very few countries in the Pacific could provide the economies of scale required for private sector operations, governments could encourage the private sector to manage certain aspects of services. There will be a growing demand for the private sector in housing development if the land supply constraints could be removed.

E. Human resource development

Trained professionals are in short supply in the fields of urban management, urban and regional planning, urban infrastructure and land development, and construction disciplines. The improvement of institutional arrangements for urban development at the central and local government levels would encourage greater interest in these professions.

The land management and development course at the University of the South Pacific, (USP) as well as the courses in architecture, civil engineering and urban and regional planning at the Papua New Guinea University of Technology (Unitech), have trained a number of professionals but more trained professionals are needed, and with a more holistic approach to human settlements development.

The USP course in land management and development has a comprehensive curriculum providing students with a choice of urban or rural focus. This course not only covers the technical subjects of land surveying, valuation, construction technology, property development and GIS but also relevant aspects of macroeconomics, commerce, accounting, law, sociology and management, together with a full coverage of the principles and problems of land tenure.

In addition to the land management and development course, USP offers a basic undergraduate course in town planning for those already working or interested in working in town and country planning without having to leave the region. However, the courses offered are running below capacity and USP is therefore unable to introduce courses to cover other aspects of human settlements management. Training is also needed in a range of skills at the technician level (for example, for electricians, plumbers and carpenters). This is being provided at national institutes in many countries in the region but the volume of trainee intakes would need to be increased to supply the demand that would be created by positive improvements in national programmes for improving urban development.

The training of local government councillors has been identified by the Commonwealth Local Government Forum as being an essential need. In the Pacific, this is a new sphere of public administration and adequate training for both elected representatives and local government personnel is essential to develop the capacity for addressing the new situations posed by growing urbanization.

Box 6. Recommendations for local government capacity-building

Local government capacity-building should be undertaken through four mechanisms:

1.　Institutional strengthening, especially in the area of capabilities in negotiating with national and provincial governments, and with local authorities. National networks of professional and local government practitioners should be established and linked forward with overseas national and regional local government associations and organizations.

2.　Improved access to and greater capacity of quality education and training programmes in all human resource management and human resource development areas. Access to international and regional universities such as Northern Territory University (NTU), University of the South Pacific, University of Papua New Guinea, and the Papua Guinea University of Technology at Lae, James Cook University, etc. should be encouraged and developed.

3.　Greater international linkages and partnerships should be fostered to exchange technical and managerial skills and knowledge between countries and organizations.

4.　Greater access to and development of information and databases and exchange of information in local government matters should be undertaken.

Source: Commonwealth Local Government Forum and South Pacific Forum: Round Table on Decentralization and Good Government at the Local Level, Pacific Region, held at Port Moresby, May 1997, recommendation C.

VI. URBAN GOVERNANCE AND MANAGEMENT

The issues briefly covered above concerning planning, infrastructure, housing, land supply and community participation need to be addressed in an integrated manner through a division of responsibilities between the central and local governments.

At the central government level this calls for a high level of coordination among the different agencies that provide services in urban centres and a proactive interest in developing the administrative capacity at the city level.

The concept of sound urban governance involves the establishment of effective management systems for the mobilization and utilization of physical, economic, cultural and human resources and for transparency and accountability to the community.

The techniques of sound urban governance have been thoroughly explored by the World Bank, UNDP and the United Nations Centre for Human Settlements under the Urban Management Programme. The principles have been applied in many cities in the developing countries through technical assistance programmes (UNCHS 1998).

A. Political commitment to urban governance

The comparative newness of the urbanization process and the scale and speed of urban growth have made it difficult for national, provincial and local governments to facilitate the supply of the key factors of urban production: land, shelter, infrastructure and services. Inadequate planning and provision of services are felt primarily by the poor, resulting in an increase in inequality within towns and cities.

Increasing demand for urban services calls for sound urban management and planning practices suited to local political and social contexts, supported with improved technical competence and financial inputs. Sound urban governance and management should be considered a crucial part of the national economic development process.

Box 7. Recommendations for successful decentralization

The following key principles are important components for successful decentralization strategies:

1. Giving formal recognition to the role of local government, including constitutional recognition and the enactment of appropriate national legislation.

2. Ensuring autonomy for local government as an equal sphere of government alongside provincial and national government.

3. Defining clearly the distinct role and functions of local government in relation to other spheres of government.

4. Establishing regular, open and democratic local elections, taking account of the respective cultural context.

5. Developing transparent and accountable local government.

6. Ensuring that local government is properly resourced.

7. Recognizing the role of traditional leaders and the relevance of local cultural diversity.

Source: Commonwealth Local Government Forum and South Pacific Forum: Round Table on Decentralization and Good Government at the Local Level, Pacific Region, held at Port Moresby, May 1997, recommendation A.

In Samoa, the seventh national development plan proposed to introduce new legislation for the establishment of an Apia municipal authority with powers to control land use, improve services and promote the economic and social development of the city. However, progress has been slow. Cook Islands also considered establishing a local authority for the urban area of Rarotonga but no concrete action has been taken. In both countries, the idea of a western-style local government is contrary to the traditional systems of leadership and customary land ownership patterns.

However, urban areas are modernizing at a fast rate and the traditional structures do not have the capacity for the kind of urban management that is needed. Perhaps a mixture of both systems could be devised with the assistance of transitions such as the Asia-Pacific section of the International Union of Local Authorities (IULA-ASPAC) and the Commonwealth Local Government Forum. The Forum identified some of the key actions necessary to decentralize power and responsibilities at its South Pacific round table, as is shown in box 7.

B. Economic reforms

The Pacific island states have some serious economic and natural constraints. These include small domestic markets and distance from larger markets, narrow resource bases, lack of economies of scale, limited domestic revenue-generating capacity, a high degree of dependence on external assistance, importance of remittances, the public sector and imports, and vulnerability to external shocks and natural disasters.

Many governments in the region are currently implementing economic and public sector reform measures coordinated by the Asian Development Bank targeted towards increases in income and employment and improvements in human development indicators. The critical goals of the reform process that could have a positive effect on the approaches to urban management are:

- Achieving macroeconomic stability.

- Instituting good governance with greater public participation in government.

- Making public service more accountable for efficient and effective service.

- Catalysing private sector investment to provide more incomes, employment, goods and services.

C. Capacity to address new challenges

Local government in the Pacific is generally based on western models in Melanesia and the Federated States of Micronesia. Under the provisions of the relevant legislation, a proposal to declare a city or a town over a defined area is publicly notified and representations are dealt with. Local elections are organized and the elected body forms the local government. Papua New Guinea and Solomon Islands have a provincial system of government, which has responsibility for local government.

In Vanuatu, the Municipalities Act of 1985 sets up municipalities with responsibilities but capacity is lacking at the local level. In Apia, in the absence of elected local government, an arrangement is made based on traditional local leadership structures of the different villages that form the urban centre.

Fiji has a well-developed system of urban local government, with two city councils and 11 town councils. In many centres, urban development has spread beyond the municipal boundaries into areas under the jurisdiction of rural local authorities. These authorities have the basic function of preserving public health and come under the supervision of a different government ministry. No district councils have been constituted for such areas under the

Local Government Act. For the administration of native affairs there is a system of provincial governments.

A general characteristic is that local government bodies of either model have insufficient capacity to manage and respond adequately to the pace of urban growth. Usually, there is a division of responsibilities and in most countries in the South Pacific major infrastructure services are provided by central government agencies and local authorities have the responsibility for management of the local environment and manage public facilities such as the markets. However, the crucial role for the local government is the planning and coordination of local and central government initiatives. Most do not have the legal authority or the financial capacity or the human resources for this essential task. This has been the experience of the Honiara Town Council in the implementation of the Honiara Town Council Development Plan 1988-1992.

Although most governments recognize the need for a decentralized form of government at the urban level, political support for the growth of local government is limited. Local councils receive limited financial support from central governments and external aid is seldom directed towards increasing local government capacity. The smallness of some countries leads to limited government interest in promoting subnational urban government, which is seen as duplication. In some countries, urban government is currently in the process of evolution and democratic processes have been introduced in recent years. The Commonwealth Local Government Forum, at its South Pacific round table, has identified a set of useful suggestions for good government at the local level.

Box 8. Recommendations for achieving good governance at the local level

Achieving good government at the local level can be achieved by paying attention to five factors:

1.   Strengthening administrative and management skills of staff through capacity-building, education and training.

2.   Financial arrangements and resource growth through resource-sharing with other government spheres and increased and expanded revenue-raising authority and capacity – there should be a freeing-up of the ability of local government to seek access to borrowings from financial institutions.

3.   Local government and community empowerment with statutory provision for greater openness and accountability with access to a local government ombudsman on state and national issues - there should also be a public education programme in local government to encourage full community participation.

4.   New mechanisms for service delivery, including more cost-effective quality service provided by local government, state/national partnerships, and greater involvement of NGOs, the private sector and community organizations, all in a context of promoting environmentally and socially sustainable development.

Achieving equal opportunities and gender balance through the encouragement and involvement of women in local government while recognizing that, as a result of natural cultural differences, transitional mechanisms may need to be put in place in the move towards a greater gender balance in local government.

Source: Commonwealth Local Government Forum and South Pacific Forum: Round Table on Decentralization and Good Government at the Local Level, held at Port Moresby, May 1997, recommendation B.

D. Urban financial base

Urban government bodies in the South Pacific operate with insufficient funds but their responsibilities are growing. Most city and town councils are barely able to finance regular service functions and have little or no reserves for undertaking minor capital works. Yet they serve a wide region beyond the municipal boundaries.

Most local government authorities are expected to mobilize their own finances and they rely largely upon property taxation raised from the area within their jurisdiction. Some have the authority to charge business licences and some, like Suva and Nadi in Fiji, have constructed commercial buildings which are being managed successfully and with positive financial results.

In countries that do not have a land-taxation regime, local authorities are totally dependent on financial support from the central government. In Apia, there is no formal local authority and no property taxes are imposed. Additionally, there is no requirement to register property developments with any government agency (UNCHS 1996b).

Local governments in the region experience many problems in the area of finance. The major ones are the collection of property rates or taxes, especially arrears, inability to collect rates on unleased customary lands and lands occupied by squatters, and political difficulties in raising rates to the maximum level permitted in the local government legislation. The tax-paying responsibilities of an urban landowner are not yet fully recognized by customary landowners in cities and towns in most countries. The land revenue base is a potential source of finance for supporting the development of local government in the South Pacific but it remains untapped. Meanwhile, the provision of services in urban areas remains a financial burden on central governments.

Local government bodies with a record of sound financial management have the possibility of accessing capital markets but this often requires a guarantee from central government. This aspect clearly demonstrates the responsibility that central governments need to discharge to encourage sound urban development. This type of central government support of a facilitating nature for local governments is required not only in the area of finance but also in the area of land supply. Effective central government initiatives are urgently required in order to activate the land market mechanisms that promote orderly urban growth. Such action can have the effect of strengthening the revenue base of local governments on a sustainable basis.

VII. REGIONAL COOPERATION

Countries have been addressing urban management problems with little information from or contact with other countries in the region or outside. Many international programmes in human settlements bypass the Pacific for a variety of reasons, including distance, relative smallness of the problems and the absence of a regional voice on human settlements issues. A regional programme in human settlements would benefit countries in the following ways:

- Increasing awareness of the problems in urbanization and the opportunities for economic and social development that sound urban management can generate.

- Enabling a collaborative approach to seek solutions.

- Providing information on the many successful experiences to improve national responses.

- Provide a unified position at global and major regional forums.

Specific items for regional collaboration include improvement of human resources in the urban development fields, urban/local government administration, customary land development, waste management and application of urban and housing indicators.

PART TWO

TOWARDS A PACIFIC HABITAT AGENDA: SUMMARY OF RECOMMENDATIONS

VIII. URBANIZATION AND PLANNING

National populations are increasing rapidly in most of the Pacific island states and an increasing proportion of the national populations is now living in urban centres. In spite of past and current emphasis on rural development, the future of human settlements in the Pacific is an urban one. This new phenomenon in the development of the Pacific islands needs to be recognized by governments as a reflection of social advancement and modernization. Urbanization has many positive social, economic and environmental aspects and these need to be addressed in an integrated manner at the national, provincial and local levels to ensure a constantly improving quality of life for people.

A. Formulating national plans for urbanization

As the Pacific island economies become more closely linked with the global economy, the pressure for efficient urban management will increase. Governments need to consider urbanization as a crucial part of the national economic development process and adopt a positive and proactive approach to urban growth by taking measures that enable towns to grow in an orderly way. This will be a departure for many governments but there is sufficient experience in the Pacific to build upon. An example of a recent national initiative is the National Plan of Action on Urbanization submitted by the Government of Papua New Guinea to the United Nations Conference on Human Settlements (Habitat II). Governments should consider formulating national plans for urbanization and include these as integral parts of the national economic development plans or similar national planning instrument.

B. Coordinating physical planning with economic planning

Most countries have undertaken medium-term strategic development planning but physical planning has been a relatively neglected area. For efficient and sustainable development, physical planning needs to be integrated or at least coordinated with economic and social development planning. This can best be achieved at the regional level to incorporate economic, social and physical planning, taking into account current and projected symbiotic relationships between the town and its surrounding areas. Such an approach would strengthen coordination between urban planning and national economic development planning. Appropriate institutional arrangements and legislation would need to be introduced suited to the national and local contexts.

C. Promoting integrated rural and regional development

The promotion of rural development is essential since a substantial proportion of the national population lives in the rural areas but these should be complemented with urban development policies. Regional cities and rural centres need to be strengthened to service the rural areas and outer islands.

IX. URBAN INFRASTRUCTURE

It is important to recognize that adequate provision of urban services is the key to orderly development of cities and, considering the high cost of investment, it is essential that existing assets are rehabilitated and maintained and that the consumer base is expanded.

A. Conserving water resources

Water resources need to be protected, especially catchment areas outside the urban areas, as well as underground water resources. Improved management practices are required to preserve the viability of existing water supply systems.

B. Providing sewerage

Proper sewerage services are essential even for normal urban densities and there is a limit to the efficiency of septic tanks in the geological conditions of urban centres such as Honiara, Port Moresby and Suva. The investment in sewerage reticulation and treatment facilities is relatively high but the long-term costs of avoiding such investments are much higher. Information also needs to be disseminated on suitable on-site technologies such as ventilated improved pit latrines, which have had some success in Vanuatu.

C. Improving solid waste management

The gravity of the problem of waste management needs to be recognized and the cultural constraints on sound waste management need to be addressed. Possible action could include the following:

- Community consultations could resolve the issue of the availability of suitable lands for waste disposal.

- Waste minimization programmes could be launched through public information.

- Waste recycling programmes could be encouraged.

D. Financing infrastructure

A number of initiatives could be undertaken to mobilize funds for the adequate provision of services. These include:

- Making better use of existing urban infrastructure investment, using community decision-making processes to clarify cost-recovery and management issues, improve arrangements for long-term maintenance and formulate investment plans.

- Encouraging the potential role of the private sector, as well as community associations and cooperatives, in building and owning categories of infrastructure, particularly in the larger island countries.

- Sharing the burden of financing between the central government and the urban local government.

- Examining the possibility of accessing provident funds, which now dominate the finance sector in most island countries, to become a regular source for infrastructure financing.

- Examining the possibility of selected urban authorities issuing bonds, under government guarantee, for financing the urban infrastructure.

X. HOUSING DEVELOPMENT

The growing level of urbanization will generate a constant demand for housing at all affordability levels. Housing is an important component of the construction industry and a recognized generator of employment opportunities. Global experience indicates that poor people build cheaper and more satisfactory houses than governments through self-help systems or through private sector initiatives. The key to solving the urban housing problem is to enable markets to produce as many solutions as possible in different physical, social and financial environments.

A. Developing local building materials

The development of local building materials could be encouraged and local building regulations could be adapted to suit local affordability levels and permit incremental construction of houses. The informal sector could have an active role.

B. Improving housing finance mechanisms

Alternative ways for developing mechanisms for housing finance include:

- Accessing members' credits with the provident fund for equity for loans provided by housing corporations, commercial banks and the development bank.

- Developing housing capital markets by encouraging the setting-up of private housing finance entities, with or without government equity. The Commonwealth Development Corporation and its local partners in the region could provide a lead in this field.

- Clan-based guarantees to housing loans, as in Samoa.

- Credit unions and similar community-based saving schemes.

- Adapting the "banking on the poor" approach of the Grameen Bank in Bangladesh and the Urban Community Development Office of the Government of Thailand, to provide small loans for housing, small businesses and services.

C. Providing secure and serviced sites for the poor

All Pacific people have the ability to construct simple shelters through the assistance of family members and friends. For this they need sites with basic services and a secure tenure, legal or customary, and small loans. Thus, the meeting of housing needs is dependent largely on improving the land supply mechanisms.

D. Upgrading informal settlements

Policies should be put in place to safeguard the housing investment that people have made in informal settlements and to upgrade such settlements by providing security of tenure through negotiation with the landowners and providing the basic services at affordable levels. The community can manage the upgrading process over time with support from the appropriate agencies and NGOs. Reviewing the mandates of national housing agencies to enable them to play a more strategic role in urban development could do this.

XI. LAND SUPPLY

Urbanization requires the availability of serviced land on a regular basis for a whole range of private and public urban uses. As most government and freehold land in and around urban centres is built up (except for government lands in Tonga), most of the land development will have to take place on customary land. Governments and landowners throughout the Pacific need to formulate ways of adapting the management of customary land to the modern opportunities and requirements of orderly urban development. Moreover, there is an urgent need to optimize the use of existing developed land through appropriate urban planning and fiscal tools.

A. Reviewing new initiatives

New land policy initiatives to adapt customary land procedures to modern needs and innovative approaches to bring land on to the market would facilitate not only orderly urban development but also economic development generally. The following experiences in the Pacific could be reviewed to this end:

- Fiji's Native Land Trust Board roles as a custodian and as a developer of customary lands.

- Landowner initiatives in the peri-urban areas of Papua New Guinea and Fiji to meet the demand by creating informal urban settlements.

- Vanuatu's initiatives in urban land reform.

B. Considering an incremental approach to land development

Land subdivision standards could be adjusted to allow incremental development of infrastructure so as to increase affordability by tenants and thus activate the land market. Under such an incremental approach only the essential services would be installed first, enabling people to settle at affordable prices. Upgrading of infrastructure can be undertaken later through a combination of central and local government and community investments.

C. Enabling customary landowners to become active in the land market

Governments could launch or support capacity-building programmes to enable customary landowners to be active in the land market. Governments could provide basic infrastructure to guide the opening-up of land for orderly settlement. Legislation could be introduced to facilitate long-term leasing of customary land, with adequate protection for landowners and tenants. Land readjustment processes could be introduced to facilitate adjoining owners of small parcels or irregularly shaped lands to be developed in an orderly manner.

D. Expanding the application of GIS

The application of GIS could be expanded to facilitate land-titling processes. This technology is also able to support all aspects of urban land management at the central and local government levels.

XII. COMMUNITY PARTICIPATION AND HUMAN RESOURCES

The people of the Pacific have demonstrated considerable skills in community participation for resolving issues of common concern through traditional leadership structures. At the urban level, community organizations, leadership structures and the issues are different and complex. People represent a vast resource and genuine public participation can resolve the crucial political and institutional issues for orderly urban development.

Human resources development will be a constant requirement as urbanization increases and the need for adequately trained personnel at the managerial, professional and technician levels cannot be underestimated.

A. Encouraging community participation and urban forums

Community participation could be encouraged in the following ways:

- Governments could support community participation by holding urban forums to establish a political process that would involve all stakeholders at the national, provincial and local levels for developing a consensus on policies and strategies for urban management.

- Women's groups can play an active role in community consultations.

- Communities and landowning groups could undertake real estate development after acquiring some knowledge and skills in subdividing land, mobilizing finance and producing and supplying building materials and organizing housing construction. They could be provided with guidance in such ventures by the relevant government agencies and NGOs.

B. Developing human resources

Sustained programmes for urban management would attract larger intakes of students in the built environment courses in the region.

- Embark on human resources development programmes to provide skills for land development, infrastructure management, physical planning, housing, financial management, local government administration and business management within the institutions existing in the region.

- A regional programme could be considered to increase human resources in these fields.

- Technician-level training at the national technical institutes could be strengthened.

- Information exchange on human settlement matters within the Pacific is currently non-existent but could be initiated.

- Opportunities could be provided for staff from one national or urban government agency to be attached to a similar agency in another country.

C. Enhancing NGO contributions

The contribution of NGOs could be enhanced through government action to remove the many constraints on their operations and by providing active support.

D. Involving the private sector in urban management

The private sector can play an active role in certain urban management operations on a cost-plus basis and there are many services which people are willing to pay for if these are reliable and efficient. Avenues for services to be provided by the private sector need to be explored in the context of each city since the economic reforms currently under implementation will tend to encourage the expansion of the private sector.

XIII. URBAN GOVERNANCE AND MANAGEMENT

The issues described above relating to planning, urban infrastructure, land and housing need to be addressed in an integrated manner since all are closely related. Appropriate institutional arrangements need to be made at the national and the urban centre level for the various aspects of the planning, development and management of urban areas, with a clear division of responsibilities and with adequate channels for effective public participation. The difficult problems in urban development (except for the investments for infrastructure) are not so much technical but political and institutional.

It may not be necessary in all the Pacific countries to have a distinct local government authority based on western models. Experience in most developing countries indicates that, after a certain size, a dedicated urban level of government is necessary to address the growing volume and complexity of issues of a local nature through representatives of the local residents. Any urban-level government will be a creature of the central government and its structure will need to take into account the social, cultural and economic context in which it is expected to deliver governance.

A. Generating commitment to good urban governance

Governments could ensure sound urban governance by:

- Creating appropriate capacity at the ministerial level for guiding the urban management process and for ensuring effective government at the urban level.

- Taking a proactive role in the development and improvement of effective local models for urban management.

- Enabling urban governments, whether of the western model of elected councillors or those based on traditional leadership structures or other models, to manage efficiently.

- Encouraging the development of transparency and accountability in urban government administrations.

- The process of generating commitment to urban governance may be achieved through a series of community consultations. Experiences in the Pacific that could be referred to include:

- Kiribati's consultation process for the formation of the Urban Management Plan for South Tarawa.

- Consultation process in Palau for the preparation of the urban plan.

B. Strengthening urban governments

Greater political support could be given to develop the capacity of urban governments by:

- Encouraging partnership programmes among different levels of government, the private sector, NGOs and community organizations.

- Providing training, facilitating dialogue on good urban government and increasing information dissemination at the national and regional levels.

- Achieving gender balance among local government representatives.

- Improving the legislative framework relating to urban government.

- Strengthening the capacity of urban government bodies to plan, develop and manage urban centres more efficiently and with greater involvement of local communities and regular upgrading of human resources.

Fiji's current review of the local government legislation for strengthening municipal management could be of interest to the region.

C. Improving urban finances

Devolving power to the local level without commensurate financial capacity is meaningless. There is a need to improve the resource base and financial management capabilities of urban governments to enable them to regularly undertake minor capital development works and to mobilize finance from capital markets for major capital works. Actions include:

- Resolving the issue of fiscal support to local governments through effective dialogue between central and local governments.

- Removing institutional and legal constraints to collection of rates.

- Exploring additional means of revenue generation, including the operation of markets and bus stations and wider collection of business licences.

- Making arrangements for the sharing of the revenue base and administration among urban authorities within the urban region.

- Enabling selected local governments to borrow development funds from capital markets.

- Generating community confidence through improved discipline in financial management.

D. Encouraging the small business and micro-enterprise sector

A proactive approach could be taken to encourage the growth of small businesses and micro-enterprises, which usually operate in the informal sector, so that they can absorb some of the unemployed. Strategies include:

- Providing serviced sites, relaxation of some regulations and provision of small loans.

- Providing technical and marketing guidance.

- Ensuring a constant programme of land development with basic infrastructure and incremental housing construction that could engage the informal sector on a regular basis.

- Setting up "weekend markets".

- Encouraging the formation of profession-based cooperatives etc.

XIV. REGIONAL COOPERATION

Countries have been addressing urban management problems with little information from or contact with other countries in the region or outside. Many international programmes in human settlements bypass the Pacific for a variety of reasons, including distance, the relative smallness of the problems and the absence of a regional voice on human settlements issues.

A regional programme in human settlements would benefit countries through:

- Increasing awareness of the problems in urbanization and the opportunities for economic and social development that sound urban management can generate.

- Enabling a collaborative approach to seeking solutions.

- Providing information on the many successful experiences to improve national responses.

- Providing a unified position at global and major regional forums.

- Improving human resources in the urban development fields, urban/local government administration, customary land development, waste management and application of urban and housing indicators.

REFERENCES

Connell J., 1999. "Urbanization and Settlement in the Pacific: Resettlement Policy and Practice in South East Asia and the Pacific: Proceedings of Workshops held in Manila and Port Vila 1998" (revised draft, Asian Development Bank).

Connell, J. and J. P. Lea, 1993. Planning the Future: Melanesian Cities in 2010, *Pacific 2010 Series* (Canberra, National Centre for Development Studies, Research School of Pacific Studies, Australian National University).

Crocombe, R. 1989.*The South Pacific: An Introduction, Fifth Revised Edition* (Suva, University of South Pacific). 5th rev. ed.

Crocombe, R. 1994. "Trends and issues in Pacific land tenure", in R. Crocombe and M. Meleisia, ed., 1994. *Land Issues in the Pacific* (Christchurch and Suva, University of Canterbury, Macmillan Brown Centre for Pacific Studies and Institute of Pacific Studies, University of the South Pacific).

ESCAP, 1991. *Report of the Consultative Meeting of National Experts in Human Settlements of Small Pacific Island Developing Countries, Port Vila, Vanuatu, 3-6 October 1990* (Bangkok).

Government of Fiji and UNDP, 1997. *Fiji Poverty Report* (Suva, United Nations Development Programme).

Country Report (Istanbul, United Nations Conference on Human Settlements).

Papua New Guinea University of Technology, 1985. *South Pacific Regional Workshop on Housing-IYSH 1987-International Year of Shelter for the Homeless* (Lae, Papua New Guinea University of Technology).

South Pacific Regional Environment Programme, 1992. *The Pacific Way: Report of Pacific Island Developing Countries to the United Nations Conference on Environment and Development* (Apia, SPREP).

United Nations, 1994. *Report of the Global Conference on the Sustainable Development of Small Island Developing States.*

United Nations Centre for Human Settlements, 1988 *Global Strategy for Shelter to the Year 2000* (Nairobi, UNCHS).

United Nations Centre for Human Settlements, 1990. *Human Settlements and Sustainable Development: The Role of Human Settlements and of Human Settlement Policies in Meeting Development Goals and in Addressing the Issues of Sustainability at the Global and Local Levels* (Nairobi, UNCHS).

United Nations Centre for Human Settlements, 1992. *Human Settlements Sector Review: Fiji* (Nairobi, UNCHS).

United Nations Centre for Human Settlements, 1993. *Human Settlements Sector Review: Papua New Guinea* (Nairobi, UNCHS).

United Nations Centre for Human Settlements, 1996a. *An Urbanizing World: Global Report on Human Settlements 1996* (Oxford University Press).

United Nations Centre for Human Settlements, 1996b. *Review of Human Settlements in Eastern Pacific Countries: Western Samoa, Cook Islands and Niue* (Nairobi and Suva, UNCHS and UNDP).

United Nations Centre for Human Settlements, 1997a. *The Istanbul Declaration and The Habitat Agenda* (Nairobi, UNCHS).

United Nations Centre for Human Settlements, 1998. *Urban Management Programme: Programme Report 1996-1997* (Nairobi, UNCHS).

United Nations Development Programme, 1994 *Pacific Human Development Report* (Suva, UNDP).

University of Queensland, 1993.*Global Strategy for Shelter to the Year 2000 South Pacific Sub-regional Seminar* (Brisbane, University of Queensland).